# knitbot *linen*

six unstructured knits

*by* hannah fettig

*published by* Quince & Co.

ISBN 9780985299033
Printed in the United States by Puritan Press

# table *of* contents

Before setting out to knit with linen, something must be understood: Knitting with linen is different than knitting with wool or other yarns spun from animal fiber. Linen is a plant fiber. This means there is no elasticity to the yarn. When knitting with wool, your stitches have bounce. Even if your tension is inconsistent, your stitches can be manipulated through blocking into a nice even fabric. Your linen stitches, however, once created, are frozen in time. No amount of attention is going to get them to be anything other than what they are.

Due to the way linen yarn twists, you may notice, too, that your knitted fabric has a bias. It slants to one side, like a trapezoid versus a square. Also, ribbing worked in linen doesn't pull in as you typically want ribbing to do.

But let's also understand why we choose to knit with linen despite its being temperamental, at times. Linen yarn creates a fabric with beautiful drape and a garment that's comfortable to wear and softens with time. It's just a different little bird, is all. If we understand its characteristics, we can create some beautiful garments for ourselves.

## Edges

One thing I like about working with linen is that stockinette stitch edges lay flat and don't have wool's tendency to roll. All of the designs in this collection are knitted with a raw edge which, if worked in wool, can roll a bit. If you're substituting wool for any of these designs you may want to work a simple rib or garter stitch border to ensure that the piece lays flat.

## Gauge

As knitters, most of us understand the importance of checking our gauge. In the case of linen, it is all the more necessary given its nature. If you're a tight or a loose knitter, this will only be exaggerated when working with this yarn. A pool of knitters working with linen may all need different needle sizes to achieve the same gauge. And so we say it again—take time to check your gauge!

## Finishing

A neat finishing job is especially important for a linen sweater. So how should you weave in those ends? First, keep in mind when it's time to begin a new skein and try to do so in an inconspicuous spot. If you're working a flat piece, start when beginning a new row, so you can weave in the ends later along the side seam. However, if you're working a cardigan, don't start a new skein at the center front edge, only at the side seam. If you're working in the round, start the new skein at a side marker, not front or back center. When it's time to weave in those ends, do so on the wrong side using a duplicate stitch.

## Wash and care

What's the best way to block your linen garment? You can hand wash and air dry flat as you most likely do with your wool pieces. To experience how soft linen can become, go ahead and throw it in the washer and dryer—just pull it out of the dryer while it's still a bit damp. Then give it a quick iron if you like or let it finish air drying. In swatch tests we've conducted, the fabric does not shrink. But to be safe, go ahead and run your swatches through the washer and dryer and see what results you get before doing the same with your finished garment. You can use your regular laundry detergent.

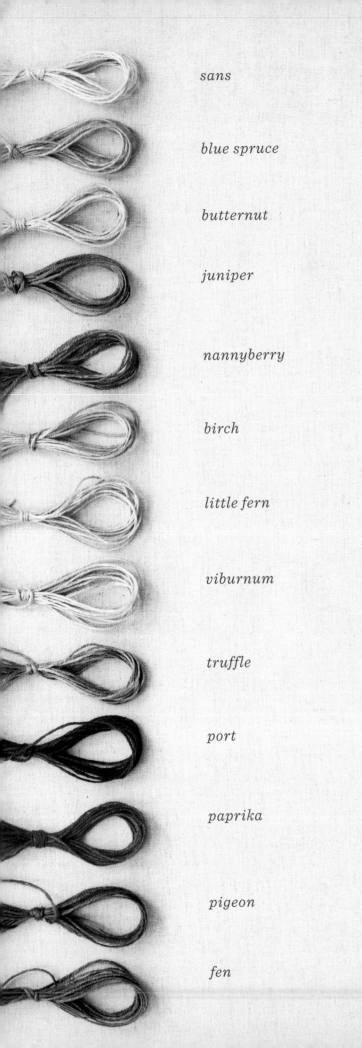

sans

blue spruce

butternut

juniper

nannyberry

birch

little fern

viburnum

truffle

port

paprika

pigeon

fen

Our linen yarn, *Sparrow*, is spun in Italy from flax grown organically in Belgium. Why, you might ask, is Quince & Company, a business dedicated to American fiber and spinners, bringing in a little brown bird from Europe?

A yarn company specializing in domestic wool needs to think about summer knitting, too, if it's to thrive. Enter *Sparrow*. We love its durability, smooth hand, and silky appearance. Could we make it here? Not hardly.

Flax, the linen plant, isn't grown commercially (yet) in the U.S. Someday we'd love to see meadows of blue flowers become part of our North American rural, or not-so-rural, landscape. (Wouldn't that be grand?)

Until then, we'll source flax from Belgium where, for centuries, through climate and experience, they've grown and processed the world's finest linen fiber. Why an Italian spinning mill? Because the one we work with has a long tradition of spinning linen to make a refined, pretty yarn. And, important for a small company, they're willing to sell us the small quantities we need.

Our first summer, we introduced *Sparrow* in one color, Sans, the yarn undyed. A soft, pale and pearly, brown.

The next season, because we love the way linen takes color, we introduced six soft vegetable-dye-inspired colors and named them after trees and plants from the White Mountains: Birch, Blue Spruce, Nannyberry, Butternut, Juniper, and Little Fern.

This summer, we've added six more colors: Port, a deep, dark winey plum, Viburnum, an icy, vintage pink, Pigeon, blue slate, Paprika, spicy, rich orange, Truffle, smokey gray-lavender, and Fen, a marshy green-brown.

Garments knitted with linen only improve with wear and washing. As nice as a *Sparrow* piece is right off the needles, over time it will soften and drape, and the color will develop a lovely patina. Knit up Hannah's pieces herein and see.

# the *patterns*

# Point of View Vest

This minimalist high back vest will add a lot of punch to your summer wardrobe. I wanted this piece to be both angular and soft at the same time. The natural drape of linen contributes to its soft feel as the vest easily falls open at the front. Worked from the bottom up, the left and and right fronts are knitted separately then joined at the back. Once the body is complete you divide for the armholes and complete the fronts and back. Finally the shoulders are seamed.

## Finished measurements
31 ½ (35, 38 ½, 42, 45 ¾, 49 ¼, 52 ¾, 56 ¼, 59 ¾)" [80 (89, 98, 106.5, 116, 125, 134, 143, 152) cm] at bust, and 20 (20 ¾, 21 ¾, 22 ½, 23 ¼, 23 ¾, 24 ½, 25 ¼, 26 ¼)" [51 (53, 55, 57, 59, 60.5, 62, 64, 66.5) cm] in length
Sample shown is 31 ½" [80 cm] with 1 ½" [4 cm] positive ease

## Yarn
Sparrow by Quince & Co.
(100% organic linen; 168yd [155m]/50g)
• 3 (3, 4, 4, 4, 4, 5, 5, 6) skeins in Pigeon 209
  Or 425 (475, 525, 575, 625, 675, 725, 800, 850) yds of fingering weight yarn

## Needles
• One 32" circular needle (circ) in size US 3 [3.25 mm]
## Or size to obtain gauge
## Notions
• Stitch markers (m)
• Stitch holders or waste yarn
• Tapestry needle
## Gauge
27 sts and 36 rows = 4" [10 cm] in stockinette stitch, after blocking.

# Vest
## Left Front
With circ and using the long-tail cast on, CO 70 (76, 82, 88, 94, 100, 106, 112, 118) sts.

Set up row: (WS) P68 (74, 80, 86, 92, 98, 104, 110, 116), place marker (pm), p2.

Next row inc row: (RS) K1, M1R, knit to m, sl m, knit to end (1 st inc'd).
Rep inc row every 4 rows 9 (10, 11, 12, 13, 14, 15, 16, 17) more times—80 (87, 94, 101, 108, 115, 122, 129, 136) sts.

Next row: (WS) Purl.
Place sts on a holder or waste yarn and set aside.

## Right front
CO 70 (76, 82, 88, 94, 100, 106, 112, 118) sts.

Set up row: (WS) P2, pm, p68 (74, 80, 86, 92, 98, 104, 110, 116).

Next row inc row: (RS) Knit to m, sl m, knit to last st, M1L, k1 (1 st inc'd).
Rep inc row every 4 rows 9 (10, 11, 12, 13, 14, 15, 16, 17) more times—80 (87, 94, 101, 108, 115, 122, 129, 136) sts.

Next row: (WS) Purl.

## Add stitches for back
Next row: (RS) Knit right front sts, then using the backward loop cast on, CO 82 (92, 102, 112, 122, 132, 142, 152, 162) sts, then knit held left front sts—242 (266, 290, 314, 338, 362, 386, 410, 434) sts: 68 (74, 80, 86, 92, 98, 104, 110, 116) sts for each front, 106 (118, 130, 142, 154, 166, 178, 190, 202) back sts.
Next row: (WS) Purl.
Work even in St st until body measures 12 (12 ½, 13, 13 ½, 14, 14, 14 ½, 15, 15 ½)" [30.5 (32, 33, 34.5, 35.5, 35.5, 37, 38, 39.5) cm] at longest point, ending after a WS row.

## Divide for armholes
Next row: (RS) *Knit to 4 (5, 6, 7, 8, 9, 10, 11, 12) sts before m, BO 8 (10, 12, 14, 16, 18, 20, 22, 24) sts, removing marker; rep from * one more time, knit to end—226 (246, 266, 286, 306, 326, 346, 366, 386) sts total: 64 (69, 74, 79, 84, 89, 94, 99, 104) sts for each front, 98 (108, 118, 128, 138, 148, 158, 168, 178) back sts.

Place back and right front sts on stitch holders or waste yarn.

## Left front

Next row: (WS) Purl.

BO 0 (0, 0, 0, 2, 2, 2, 2, 2) sts at beg of next 0 (0, 0, 0, 1, 2, 3, 4, 5) RS rows—64 (69, 74, 79, 82, 85, 88, 91, 94) sts.

Next row *dec row:* (RS) K1, ssk, knit to end (1 st dec'd). Rep *dec row* every RS row 4 (6, 8, 12, 14, 15, 16, 17, 18) more times, then every 4 rows 1 (1, 1, 0, 0, 0, 0, 0, 0) times—58 (61, 64, 66, 67, 69, 71, 73, 75) sts.

Work even until armhole measures 3 ¼ (3 ¼, 3 ½, 3 ¾, 3 ¾, 4 ¼, 4 ¼, 4 ½, 4 ¾)" [8 (8, 9, 9.5, 9.5, 11, 11, 11.5, 12) cm], ending after a RS row.

### Shape neck

Next row: (WS) BO 18 sts, purl to end—40 (43, 46, 48, 49, 51, 53, 55, 57) sts.
Next row *dec row:* (RS) Knit to last 3 sts, k2tog, k1 (1 st dec'd).
Rep *dec row* every RS row 19 (20, 21, 22, 22, 23, 24, 24, 25) more times—20 (22, 24, 25, 26, 27, 28, 30, 31) sts.

Next row: (WS) Purl.
Next row: BO 10 (11, 12, 13, 13, 14, 14, 15, 16) sts, knit to end.
Next row: BO rem 10 (11, 12, 12, 13, 13, 14, 15, 15) sts.

## Right front

Place right front sts on needle, ready to work a WS row.

BO 0 (0, 0, 0, 2, 2, 2, 2, 2) sts at beg of next 0 (0, 0, 0, 1, 2, 3, 4, 5) WS rows—64 (69, 74, 79, 82, 85, 88, 91, 94) sts.

Next row *dec row:* (RS) Knit to 3 sts from end, k2tog, k1 (1 st dec'd).
Rep *dec row* every RS row 4 (6, 8, 12, 14, 15, 16, 17, 18) more times, then every 4 rows 1 (1, 1, 0, 0, 0, 0, 0, 0) times—58 (61, 64, 66, 67, 69, 71, 73, 75) sts.

Work even until armhole measures 3 ¼ (3 ¼, 3 ½, 3 ¾, 3 ¾, 4 ¼, 4 ¼, 4 ½, 4 ¾)" [8 (8, 9, 9.5, 9.5, 11, 11, 11.5, 12) cm], ending after a WS row.

### Shape neck

Next row: (RS) BO 18 sts, knit to end—40 (43, 46, 48, 49, 51, 53, 55, 57) sts.
Next row: (WS) Purl to end.
Next row *dec row:* (RS) K1, ssk, knit to end (1 st dec'd).
Rep *dec row* every RS row 19 (20, 21, 22, 22, 23, 24, 24, 25) more times—20 (22, 24, 25, 26, 27, 28, 30, 31) sts.

Next row: (WS) BO 10 (11, 12, 13, 13, 14, 14, 15, 16) sts, knit to end.

Next row: (RS) BO rem 10 (11, 12, 12, 13, 13, 14, 15, 15) sts.

## Back

Place back sts back on needle, ready to work a WS row.
Next row: (WS) Purl.
BO 2 sts at beg of next 0 (0, 0, 0, 2, 4, 6, 8, 10) rows— 98 (108, 118, 128, 134, 140, 146, 152, 158) sts.
Next row *dec row:* (RS) K1, ssk, knit to last 3 sts, k2tog, k1 (2 sts dec'd).
Rep *dec row* every RS row 4 (6, 8, 12, 14, 15, 16, 17, 18) more times, then every 4 rows 1 (1, 1, 0, 0, 0, 0, 0, 0) times—86 (92, 98, 102, 104, 108, 112, 116, 120) sts.

Cont as est until back measures 7 ½ (7 ¾, 8 ¼, 8 ½, 8 ¾, 9 ¼, 9 ½, 9 ¾, 10 ¼)" [19 (19.5, 21, 21.5, 22, 23.5, 24, 25, 26) cm] from beg of armhole, ending after a WS row.

**Next row:** (RS) K22 (24, 26, 27, 28, 29, 30, 32, 33), place these sts on a holder or waste yarn for right shoulder, BO 42 (44, 46, 48, 48, 50, 52, 52, 54) sts, knit to end.

## Left shoulder
**Row 1:** (WS) Purl.
**Row 2** *dec row:* (RS) K1, ssk, knit to end (1 st dec'd).
Rep Rows 1 and 2 one more time—20 (22, 24, 25, 26, 27, 28, 30, 31) sts.

**Next row:** (WS) BO 10 (11, 12, 13, 13, 14, 14, 15, 16) sts, purl to end.
**Next row:** BO rem 10 (11, 12, 12, 13, 13, 14, 15, 15) sts.

## Right shoulder
Place sts back on needle, ready to work a RS row.

**Row 1** *dec row:* (RS) Knit to last 3 sts, k2tog, k1 (1 st dec'd).
**Row 2:** (WS) Purl.
Rep Rows 1 and 2 one more time—20 (22, 24, 25, 26, 27, 28, 30, 31) sts.

**Next row:** (RS) BO 10 (11, 12, 13, 13, 14, 14, 15, 16) sts, knit to end.
**Next row:** BO rem 10 (11, 12, 12, 13, 13, 14, 15, 15) sts.

## Finishing
Weave in all ends. Block to measurements. Seam shoulders.

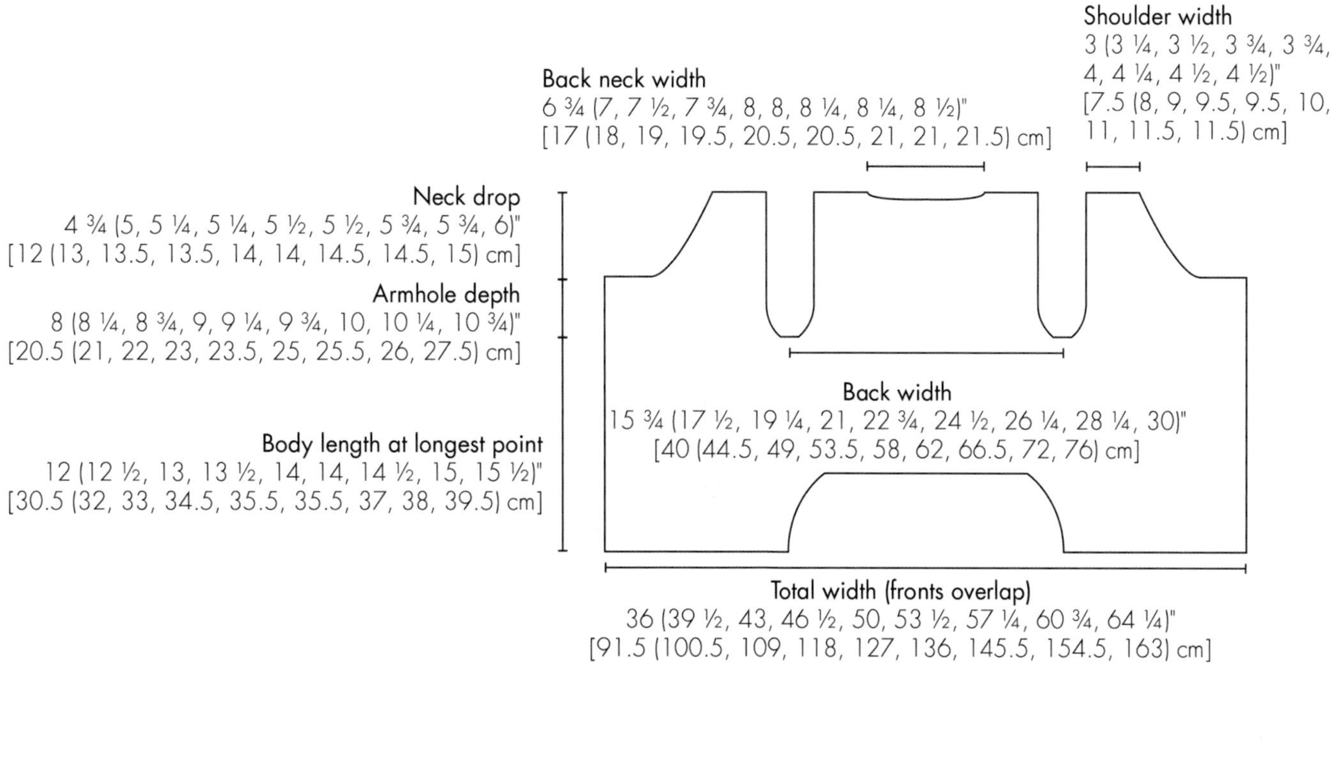

Shoulder width
3 (3 ¼, 3 ½, 3 ¾, 3 ¾, 4, 4 ¼, 4 ½, 4 ½)"
[7.5 (8, 9, 9.5, 9.5, 10, 11, 11.5, 11.5) cm]

Back neck width
6 ¾ (7, 7 ½, 7 ¾, 8, 8, 8 ¼, 8 ¼, 8 ½)"
[17 (18, 19, 19.5, 20.5, 20.5, 21, 21, 21.5) cm]

Neck drop
4 ¾ (5, 5 ¼, 5 ¼, 5 ½, 5 ½, 5 ¾, 5 ¾, 6)"
[12 (13, 13.5, 13.5, 14, 14, 14.5, 14.5, 15) cm]

Armhole depth
8 (8 ¼, 8 ¾, 9, 9 ¼, 9 ¾, 10, 10 ¼, 10 ¾)"
[20.5 (21, 22, 23, 23.5, 25, 25.5, 26, 27.5) cm]

Body length at longest point
12 (12 ½, 13, 13 ½, 14, 14, 14 ½, 15, 15 ½)"
[30.5 (32, 33, 34.5, 35.5, 35.5, 37, 38, 39.5) cm]

Back width
15 ¾ (17 ½, 19 ¼, 21, 22 ¾, 24 ½, 26 ¼, 28 ¼, 30)"
[40 (44.5, 49, 53.5, 58, 62, 66.5, 72, 76) cm]

Total width (fronts overlap)
36 (39 ½, 43, 46 ½, 50, 53 ½, 57 ¼, 60 ¾, 64 ¼)"
[91.5 (100.5, 109, 118, 127, 136, 145.5, 154.5, 163) cm]

# Lineal Cardigan

Lineal has the spirit of my signature unstructured cardigans. It also features angular shaping on the fronts and elbow length sleeves, which makes it especially right for warmer weather. It's perfect to pair with a tank or a pretty summer dress. This cardigan is worked from the top down. The collar is picked up and knitted last.

## Finished measurements

30 ¼ (33 ¾, 37 ¼, 41, 44 ½, 48, 51 ½, 55, 58 ¾)" [77 (86, 94.5, 104, 113, 122, 131, 140, 149) cm] at bust, and 19 (20 ¼, 21 ¾, 23, 24 ¾, 26, 27 ½, 28 ¾, 30 ¼)" [48.5 (51.5, 55, 58.5, 62.5, 66, 70, 72.5, 76.5) cm] in length

Sample shown is 30 ¼" [77 cm] with no ease

## Yarn

Sparrow by Quince & Co.

(100% organic linen; 168yd [155m]/50g)

- 5 (6, 7, 8, 9, 10, 11, 12, 13) skeins in Nannyberry 203 Or 800 (925, 1075, 1200, 1375, 1525, 1700, 1900, 2050) yds of fingering weight yarn

## Needles

- One 32" circular needle (circ) in size US 3 [3.25 mm]
- One set double-pointed needles (dpns) in size US 3 [3.25 mm]

Or size to obtain gauge

## Notions

- Stitch markers (m)
- Stitch holders or waste yarn
- Tapestry needle

## Gauge

27 sts and 36 rows = 4" [10 cm] in stockinette stitch, after blocking.

## Cardigan
### Begin at top

With circ and using the long-tail cast on, CO 62 (64, 66, 68, 70, 72, 74, 76, 78) sts.

**Set up row:** (WS) P2, place marker (pm), p10, pm, p38 (40, 42, 44, 46, 48, 50, 52, 54), pm, p10, pm, p2.

Work two rows even in St st.

**Row 1:** (RS) (Knit to 1 st before m, M1R, k1, sl m, k1, M1L) 4 times, knit to end (8 sts inc'd)—70 (72, 74, 76, 78, 80, 82, 84, 86) sts.

**Row 2:** (WS) Purl.

Rep these two rows 13 (14, 15, 16, 17, 18, 19, 20, 21) more times—174 (184, 194, 204, 214, 224, 234, 244, 254) sts: 16 (17, 18, 19, 20, 21, 22, 23, 24) front sts, 38 (40, 42, 44, 46, 48, 50, 52, 54) sleeve sts, 66 (70, 74, 78, 82, 86, 90, 94, 98) back sts.

**Row 1:** (RS) Knit to m, sl m, (k1, M1L, knit to 1 st before m, M1R, k1, sl m) 3 times, knit to end (6 sts inc'd)—180 (190, 200, 210, 220, 230, 240, 250, 260) sts.

**Row 2:** (WS) Purl to end.

**Row 3:** (Knit to 1 st before m, M1R, k1, sl m, k1, M1L) 4 times, knit to end (8 sts inc'd)—188 (198, 208, 218, 228, 238, 248, 258, 268) sts.

**Row 4:** Purl to end.

Rep these four rows 3 (4, 5, 6, 7, 8, 9, 10, 11) more times—230 (254, 278, 302, 326, 350, 374, 398, 422) sts: 20 (22, 24, 26, 28, 30, 32, 34, 36) front sts, 54 (60, 66, 72, 78, 84, 90, 96, 102) sleeve sts, 82 (90, 98, 106, 114, 122, 130, 138, 146) back sts.

Work 2 (0, 0, 0, 0, 0, 0, 0, 0) rows even.

**Next row** *inc row:* (RS) (Knit to 1 st before m, M1R, k1, sl m, k1, M1L) 4 times, knit to end (8 sts inc'd)—238 (262, 286, 310, 334, 358, 382, 406, 430) sts.

Rep *inc row* every RS row 0 (1, 1, 2, 2, 3, 3, 4, 4) more times, then every 4th row 4 (3, 3, 2, 2, 1, 1, 0, 0) times—270 (294, 318, 342, 366, 390, 414, 438, 462) sts: 25 (27, 29, 31, 33, 35, 37, 39, 41) front sts, 64 (70, 76, 82, 88, 94, 100, 106, 112) sleeve sts, 92 (100, 108, 116, 124, 132, 140, 148, 156) back sts.

Work 3 (3, 3, 3, 3, 3, 3, 1, 1) rows even.

## Divide sleeves from body

**Next row:** (RS) K25 (27, 29, 31, 33, 35, 37, 39, 41) left front sts, place 64 (70, 76, 82, 88, 94, 100, 106, 112) sleeve sts on a stitch holder or waste yarn, using the backward loop cast on, CO 10 (14, 18, 22, 26, 30, 34, 38, 42) sts, k92 (100, 108, 116, 124, 132, 140, 148, 156) back sts, place 64 (70, 76, 82, 88, 94, 100, 106, 112) sleeve sts on a stitch holder or waste yarn, using the backward loop cast on, CO 10 (14, 18, 22, 26, 30, 34, 38, 42) sts, k25 (27, 29, 31, 33, 35, 37, 39, 41) right front sts—162 (182, 202, 222, 242, 262, 282, 302, 322) sts.

Work even in St st until piece measures 4" [10 cm] from underarm, ending after a WS row.

**Next row** *dec row:* (RS) K1, ssk, knit to last 3 sts, k2tog, k1 (2 sts dec'd)—160 (180, 200, 220, 240, 260, 280, 300, 320) sts.
Rep *dec row* every RS row 29 (33, 37, 41, 45, 49, 53, 57, 61) more times—102 (114, 126, 138, 150, 162, 174, 186, 198) sts.

**Next row:** (WS) BO all sts loosely purlwise.

## Sleeves

Slip held sleeve sts onto dpns. With RS facing, knit 64 (70, 76, 82, 88, 94, 100, 106, 112) sleeve sts, then pick up and knit 10 (14, 18, 22, 26, 30, 34, 38, 42) sts along cast on sts at underarm, placing marker in the middle of picked up sts. Join for working in the rnd—74 (84, 94, 104, 114, 124, 134, 144, 154) sts.

Work even until sleeve measures 7 ½" [19 cm] from underarm.

Work in k1, p1 rib for 10 rnds.

**Next rnd:** BO all sts loosely in rib.

## Collar

With RS facing and starting at right front edge where decreases begin, pick up and knit sts 3 sts for every 4 rows. Cont across the top of the right sleeve, across the back, then across the top of the left sleeve, picking up 1 st for every st. Finish by picking up 3 sts for every 4 rows along left front edge, ending where decreases begin.

Beginning with a purl row, work collar in St st until collar measures 2 ½" [6.5 cm] or desired length, ending after a WS row.

**Next row:** BO all sts loosely knitwise.

## Finishing

Weave in all ends. Block to measurements.

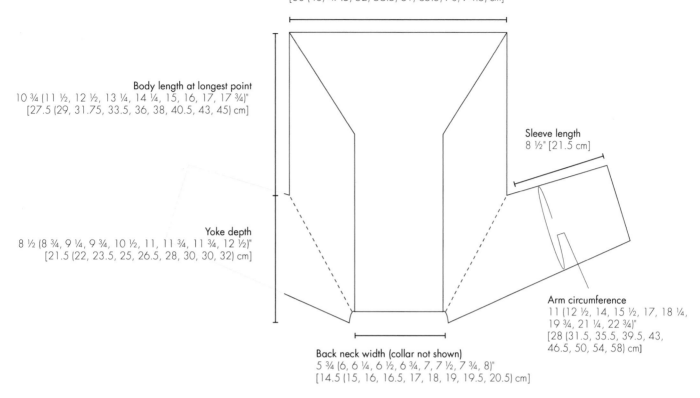

Back width
15 (17, 18 ¾, 20 ½, 22 ¼, 24, 25 ¾, 27 ½, 29 ¼)"
[38 (43, 47.5, 52, 56.5, 61, 65.5, 70, 74.5) cm]

Body length at longest point
10 ¾ (11 ½, 12 ½, 13 ¼, 14 ¼, 15, 16, 17, 17 ¾)"
[27.5 (29, 31.75, 33.5, 36, 38, 40.5, 43, 45) cm]

Sleeve length
8 ½" [21.5 cm]

Yoke depth
8 ½ (8 ¾, 9 ¼, 9 ¾, 10 ½, 11, 11 ¾, 11 ¾, 12 ½)"
[21.5 (22, 23.5, 25, 26.5, 28, 30, 30, 32) cm]

Arm circumference
11 (12 ½, 14, 15 ½, 17, 18 ¼,
19 ¾, 21 ¼, 22 ¾)"
[28 (31.5, 35.5, 39.5, 43,
46.5, 50, 54, 58) cm]

Back neck width (collar not shown)
5 ¾ (6, 6 ¼, 6 ½, 6 ¾, 7, 7 ½, 7 ¾, 8)"
[14.5 (15, 16, 16.5, 17, 18, 19, 19.5, 20.5) cm]

19

# Brise Cardigan

Here's a go-to piece for the summer months: Brise, a cardigan whose body and sleeves have just enough flow. With even less structure than Lineal, Brise has lovely movement and drape. Knitted from the top down, the slightly flared elbow length sleeves are both flattering and comfortable to wear in warmer weather. The collar is picked up and knitted last.

## Finished measurement

35 ¼ (38, 40 ¾, 43 ¼, 46, 48 ¾, 51 ¼, 54, 56 ¾, 59 ¼)" [89.5 (96.5, 103.5, 110, 117, 124, 130, 137, 144, 150.5) cm] at bust, and 21 ¾ (22 ¾, 23 ¾, 24 ¾, 25 ½, 26 ½, 27 ½, 28 ½, 29 ½, 30 ¼)" [55.5 (58, 60.5, 62.5, 65, 67.5, 70, 72, 74.5, 77) cm] in length
Sample shown is 35 ¼" [89.5 cm] with 5 ¼" positive ease

## Yarn

Sparrow by Quince & Co.
(100% organic linen; 168yd [155m]/50g)
• 7 (8, 9, 10, 11, 12, 12, 13, 14, 15) skeins in Juniper 201
  Or 1175 (1300, 1450, 1575, 1725, 1875, 2025, 2175, 2350, 2525) yds of fingering weight yarn

## Needles

• One 32" circular needle (circ) in size US 4 [3.5 mm]
• One set double-pointed needles (dpns) in size US 4 [3.5 mm]
Or size to obtain gauge

## Notions

• Stitch markers (m)
• Stitch holders or waste yarn
• Tapestry needle

## Gauge

24 sts and 36 rows = 4" in stockinette stitch, after blocking.

## Notes

This cardigan is worked from the top down, with the collar picked up from the neck edge at the end.

# Cardigan

## Begin at top

With circ and using the long-tail cast on, CO 78 (80, 82, 84, 86, 88, 90, 92, 94, 96) sts.
**Set up row:** (WS) P4 for front, place marker (pm), p12 for sleeve, pm, p46 (48, 50, 52, 54, 56, 58, 60, 62, 64) for back, pm, p12 for sleeve, pm, p4 for front.
**Row 1** *inc row:* (RS) *K1, M1L, knit to 1 st before m, M1R, k1, sl m; rep from * to last m, knit to 1 st before end, M1R, k1 (10 sts inc'd)—88 (90, 92, 94, 96, 98, 100, 102, 104, 106) sts.
**Row 2:** (WS) Purl to end.
Rep last two rows 26 (28, 30, 32, 34, 36, 38, 40, 42, 44) more times—348 (370, 392, 414, 436, 458, 480, 502, 524, 546) sts: 58 (62, 66, 70, 74, 78, 82, 86, 90, 94) sts for each front, 66 (70, 74, 78, 82, 86, 90, 94, 98, 102) sleeve sts, 100 (106, 112, 118, 124, 130, 136, 142, 148, 154) back sts.

**Next row:** (RS) Knit to end of row, then using backward loop cast on, CO 15 (16, 17, 18, 19, 20, 21, 22, 23, 24) sts.
**Next row:** (WS) Purl to end, then using backward loop cast on, CO 15 (16, 17, 18, 19, 20, 21, 22, 23, 24) sts—378 (402, 426, 450, 474, 498, 522, 546, 570, 594) sts: 73 (78, 83, 88, 93, 98, 103, 108, 113, 118) front sts, 66 (70, 74, 78, 82, 86, 90, 94, 98, 102) sleeve sts, 100 (106, 112, 118, 124, 130, 136, 142, 148, 154) back sts.

## Divide sleeves from body

**Next row:** (RS) *Knit to marker, place sleeve sts on a stitch holder or waste yarn, removing markers, CO 3 (4, 5, 6, 7, 8, 9, 10, 11, 12) sts, pm, CO 3 (4, 5, 6, 7, 8, 9, 10, 11, 12) sts, rep from * one more time, knit to end—258 (278, 298, 318, 338, 358, 378, 398, 418, 438) sts.

Cont in St st until body measures 14 ½ (15, 15 ½, 16, 16 ½, 17, 17 ½, 18, 18 ½, 19)" [37 (38, 39.5, 40.5, 42, 43, 44.5, 46, 47, 48) cm] from underarm, or desired length. BO all sts.

## Sleeves

Transfer 66 (70, 74, 78, 82, 86, 90, 94, 98, 102) sleeve sts to dpns, distributing sts evenly over 4 dpns. Knit to end, then pick up and knit 6 (8, 10, 12, 14, 16, 18, 20, 22, 24) CO sts at underarm, placing marker at center of picked up sts. Join for working in the rnd—72 (78, 84, 90, 96, 102, 108, 114, 120, 126) sts.

Work in St st for 8 rnds.

**Next rnd** *inc rnd:* K1, M1L, knit to last st before m, M1R, k1 (2 sts inc'd).
Rep *inc rnd* every 9 rnds six more times—86 (92, 98, 104, 110, 116, 122, 128, 134, 140) sts.

Cont in St st until sleeve measures 8 ½" [21.5 cm] or desired length.
**Next rnd:** BO all sts.

## Collar

With circ and starting at the right front neck, pick up and knit sts evenly along the neck edge across the right front, across the top of the sleeve, across the back, across the left sleeve, then across the left front.

Work in St st for 3" [7.5 cm], or desired length, ending after a WS row. BO all sts knitwise.

## Finishing

Weave in all ends. Block to measurements.

Total width of piece
43 (46.5, 49.75, 53, 56.25, 59.75, 63, 66.25, 69.75, 73)"
[109 (117.5, 126, 134.5, 143, 151.5, 160, 168.5, 177, 185.5) cm]

Upper arm circumference
12 (13, 14, 15, 16, 17, 18, 19, 20, 21)"
[30.5 (33, 35.5, 38, 40.5, 43,
46, 48, 51, 53.5) cm]

Body length
14½ (15, 15½, 16, 16½,
17, 17½, 18, 18½, 19)"
[37 (38, 39.5, 40.5, 42,
43, 44.5, 46, 47, 48) cm]

Cuff circumference
14¼ (15¼, 16¼, 17¼, 18¼, 19¼, 20¼, 21¼, 22¼, 23¼)"
[36 (39, 41, 44, 46.5, 49, 51.5, 54, 56.5, 59) cm]

Yoke depth
6¼ (6¾, 7¼, 7¾, 8,
8½, 9, 9½, 10, 10¼)"
[16 (17, 18.5, 20, 20.5,
21.5, 23, 24, 25.5, 26) cm]

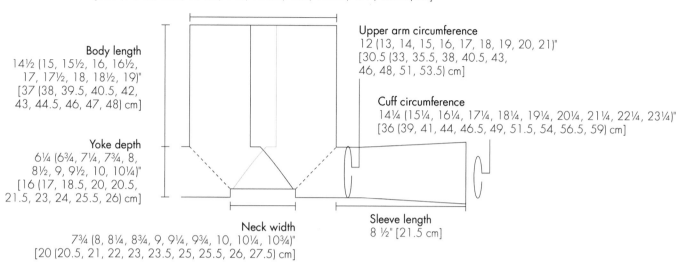

Neck width
7¾ (8, 8¼, 8¾, 9, 9¼, 9¾, 10, 10¼, 10¾)"
[20 (20.5, 21, 22, 23, 23.5, 25, 25.5, 26, 27.5) cm]

Sleeve length
8 ½" [21.5 cm]

# Aproned Tank

This tank features a narrow placket of stockinette stitch outlined in a simple border of purl stitches. The front and back are worked separately then seamed. It buttons in the back at the top of a keyhole opening.

## Finished measurements

32 (35 ¼, 39, 42 ¾, 46 ¼, 49 ¾, 53 ¼, 57)" [81 (89.5, 99, 108.5, 117.5, 126.5, 135, 145) cm] bust circumference, and 27 (28, 29, 30, 31, 32, 33, 34)" [68.5 (71, 73.5, 76, 79, 81, 84, 86.5) cm] in length
Sample shown is 32" [81 cm] with 2" [5 cm] positive ease

## Yarn

### Sparrow by Quince & Co.
(100% organic linen; 168yd [155m]/50g)
- 6 (6, 7, 8, 9, 9, 10, 11) skeins in Truffle 211
  Or 900 (1025, 1125, 1250, 1400, 1525, 1675, 1800) yds of fingering weight yarn

## Needles
- One 32" circular needle (circ) in size US 3 [3.25 mm]

**Or size to obtain gauge**

## Notions
- Stitch markers (m)
- Stitch holders or waste yarn
- Tapestry needle
- One button, ⅜" [1 cm] or larger
- One crochet hook in size US D-3
- Sewing needle and thread

## Gauge

27 sts and 36 rows = 4" [10 cm] in stockinette stitch, after blocking.

# Tank
## Back

With circ and using the long-tail cast on, CO 134 (146, 158, 170, 182, 194, 206, 218) sts.

Work in St st for 12 rows, ending after a WS row.

**Next row** *dec row:* (RS) K2, ssk, knit to last 4 sts, k2tog, k2 (2 sts dec'd)—132 (144, 156, 168, 180, 192, 204, 216) sts.
Rep *dec row* every 12th row 12 more times—108 (120, 132, 144, 156, 168, 180, 192) sts.

Work even until back measures 19 (19 ½, 20, 20 ½, 21, 21 ½, 22, 22 ½)" [48.5 (49.5, 51, 52, 53.5, 54.5, 56, 57) cm] from CO edge, ending after a WS row.

## Begin armhole shaping

BO 26 (30, 34, 38, 42, 46, 50, 54) sts at beginning of next 2 rows—56 (60, 64, 68, 72, 76, 80, 84) sts.

**Next row** *dec row:* (RS) K1, ssk, knit to last 3 sts, k2tog, k1 (2 sts dec'd)—54 (58, 62, 66, 70, 74, 78, 82) sts.
Rep *dec row* every 4 rows 2 (2, 3, 3, 4, 4, 5, 5) more times—50 (54, 56, 60, 62, 66, 68, 72) sts.

Work even until armhole measures 4 (4, 4 ½, 4 ½, 5, 5, 5 ½, 5 ½)" [10 (10, 11.5, 11.5, 13, 13, 14, 14) cm], ending after a WS row.

**Next row:** (RS) K25 (27, 28, 30, 31, 33, 34, 36), turn. Place remaining sts on a holder or waste yarn for left shoulder.

## Right shoulder

**Next row:** (WS) Purl to end.
**Next row** *dec row:* (RS) Knit to last 3 sts, k2tog, k1 (1 st dec'd).
Rep *dec row* every RS row two more times—22 (24, 25, 27, 28, 30, 31, 33) sts.

Work even until armhole measures 7 ½ (8, 8 ½, 9, 9 ½, 10, 10 ½, 11)" [19 (20.5, 21.5, 23, 24, 25.5, 26.5, 28) cm].

**Next row** *inc row:* (RS) Knit to last st, M1R, k1 (1 st inc'd).
Rep *inc row* every RS row two more times—25 (27, 28, 30, 31, 33, 34, 36) sts.

**Next row:** (WS) BO 9 (10, 10, 11, 11, 12, 12, 13) sts, purl to end.
**Next row:** BO 8 (8, 9, 9, 10, 10, 11, 11) sts, knit to end.

**Next row:** BO rem 8 (9, 9, 10, 10, 11, 11, 12) sts.

## Left shoulder
Place held sts back on needle, ready to work a RS row.
**Next row** *dec row:* (RS) K1, ssk, knit to end (1 st dec'd).
Rep *dec row* every RS row two more times—22 (24, 25, 27, 28, 30, 31, 33) sts.

Work even until armhole measures 7 ½ (8, 8 ½, 9, 9 ½, 10, 10 ½, 11)" [19 (20.5, 21.5, 23, 24, 25.5, 26.5, 28) cm].

**Next row** *inc row:* (RS) K1, M1L, knit to end (1 st inc'd).
Rep *inc row* every RS row two more times—25 (27, 28, 30, 31, 33, 34, 36) sts.

**Next row:** (WS) Purl to end.
**Next row:** BO 9 (10, 10, 11, 11, 12, 12, 13) sts, knit to end.
**Next row:** BO 8 (8, 9, 9, 10, 10, 11, 11) sts, purl to end.
**Next row:** BO rem 8 (9, 9, 10, 10, 11, 11, 12) sts.

## Front
CO 47 (52, 56, 61, 65, 70, 74, 79) sts, pm, CO 40 (42, 46, 48, 52, 54, 58, 60) sts, pm, CO 47 (52, 56, 61, 65, 70, 74, 79) sts—134 (146, 158, 170, 182, 194, 206, 218) sts.

Work in St st for 12 rows, ending after a WS row.

**Next row** *dec row:* (RS) K2, ssk, knit to last 4 sts, k2tog, k2 (2 sts dec'd).
Rep *dec row* every 12 rows 12 more times—108 (120, 132, 144, 156, 168, 180, 192) sts.

**At the same time**, when piece measures 15 (15, 15 ½, 15 ½, 16, 16, 16 ½, 16 ½)" [38 (38, 39.5, 39.5, 40.5, 40.5, 42, 42) cm], work as follows:

**Set up row:** (RS) Knit to m, sl m, purl to next m, sl m, knit to end.
**Next row:** Purl to m, sl m, k1, purl to 1 st before m, k1, sl m, purl to end.
**Next row:** Knit to m, sl m, p1, knit to 1 st before m, p1, sl m, knit to end.
Cont as est until piece measures 19 (19 ½, 20, 20 ½, 21, 21 ½, 22, 22 ½)" [48.5 (49.5, 51, 52, 53.5, 54.5, 56, 57) cm], ending after a WS row.

## Begin armhole shaping
BO 26 (30, 34, 38, 42, 46, 50, 54) sts at beg of next 2 rows—56 (60, 64, 68, 72, 76, 80, 84) sts.
**Next row** *dec row:* (RS) K1, ssk, work to last 3 sts, k2tog, k1 (2 sts dec'd).
Rep *dec row* every 4 rows 5 more times—44 (48, 52, 56, 60, 64, 68, 72) sts.

Work even until armhole measures 4 (4, 4 ½, 4 ½, 5, 5, 5 ½, 5 ½)" [10 (10, 11.5, 11.5, 13, 13, 14, 14) cm], ending after a WS row.

**Next row:** (RS) Work 18 (20, 21, 23, 24, 26, 27, 29) sts as est, BO center 8 (8, 10, 10, 12, 12, 14, 14) sts, work to end. Place left shoulder sts on a stitch holder or waste yarn.

## Right shoulder
Work 1 WS row as est.
**Next row** *dec row:* (RS) K1, ssk, knit to end (1 st dec'd).
Rep *dec row* every RS row 1 (2, 2, 3, 3, 4, 4, 5) more times—16 (17, 18, 19, 20, 21, 22, 23) sts.
Work 1 WS row as est.

**Next row:** (RS) K1, ssk, knit to last st, M1L, k1.
Rep this row every 4th row 4 more times.

Cont as est until armhole measures 8 (8 ½, 9, 9 ½, 10, 10 ½, 11, 11 ½)" [20.5 (21.5, 23, 24, 25.5, 26.5, 28, 29) cm], ending after a RS row.

**Next row:** (WS) BO 8 (8, 9, 9, 10, 10, 11, 11) sts, purl to end.
**Next row:** BO rem 8 (9, 9, 10, 10, 11, 11, 12) sts.

## Left shoulder

Place sts back on needle, ready to work a WS row.
Work 1 WS row as est.
**Next row** *dec row:* (RS) Knit to last 3 sts, k2tog, k1 (1 st dec'd).
Rep *dec row* every RS row 1 (2, 2, 3, 3, 4, 4, 5) more times—16 (17, 18, 19, 20, 21, 22, 23) sts.

Work 1 WS row as est.

**Next row:** (RS) K1, M1R, knit to last 3 sts, k2tog, k1.
Rep this row every 4th row 4 more times.

Cont as est until armhole measures 8 (8 ½, 9, 9 ½, 10, 10 ½, 11, 11 ½)" [20.5 (21.5, 23, 24, 25.5, 26.5, 28, 29) cm], ending after a WS row.

**Next row:** (RS) BO 8 (8, 9, 9, 10, 10, 11, 11) sts, knit to end.
**Next row:** BO rem 8 (9, 9, 10, 10, 11, 11, 12) sts.

## Finishing

Seam shoulders. Weave in all ends. Block to measurements. Sew on button. Using crochet hook and starting at the neck edge corner of the right back shoulder, pull a loop of yarn through the fabric and ch until chain is 1 ¼" [3 cm] or desired length, depending on the diameter of your button. Cut yarn and pull through the last ch. Securely attach this end of the chain to the other end. Weave in all ends.

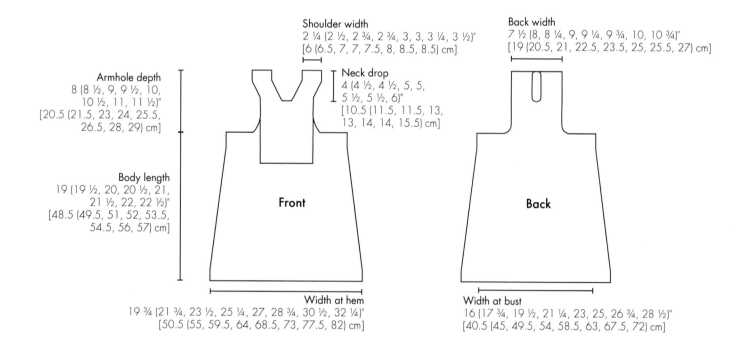

**Shoulder width**
2 ¼ (2 ½, 2 ¾, 2 ¾, 3, 3, 3 ¼, 3 ½)"
[6 (6.5, 7, 7, 7.5, 8, 8.5, 8.5) cm]

**Back width**
7 ½ (8, 8 ¼, 9, 9 ¼, 9 ¾, 10, 10 ¾)"
[19 (20.5, 21, 22.5, 23.5, 25, 25.5, 27) cm]

**Neck drop**
4 (4 ½, 4 ½, 5, 5, 5 ½, 5 ½, 6)"
[10.5 (11.5, 11.5, 13, 13, 14, 14, 15.5) cm]

**Armhole depth**
8 (8 ½, 9, 9 ½, 10, 10 ½, 11, 11 ½)"
[20.5 (21.5, 23, 24, 25.5, 26.5, 28, 29) cm]

**Body length**
19 (19 ½, 20, 20 ½, 21, 21 ½, 22, 22 ½)"
[48.5 (49.5, 51, 52, 53.5, 54.5, 56, 57) cm]

Front

Back

**Width at hem**
19 ¾ (21 ¾, 23 ½, 25 ¼, 27, 28 ¾, 30 ½, 32 ¼)"
[50.5 (55, 59.5, 64, 68.5, 73, 77.5, 82) cm]

**Width at bust**
16 (17 ¾, 19 ½, 21 ¼, 23, 25, 26 ¾, 28 ½)"
[40.5 (45, 49.5, 54, 58.5, 63, 67.5, 72) cm]

# Surrounding Tank

Interesting shaping contributes to the beautiful drape of this loose-knit, cowl-necked tank. Knitted from the top down, both decreases and increases are strategically worked when knitting the cowl-neck. Then, neck shaping creates a gusset that acts like a bust dart. The body is finally worked in the round.

## Finished measurements
33 ¼ (36 ¾, 40, 43 ¼, 46 ¾, 50, 53 ¼, 56 ¾)" [84.5 (93.5, 101.5, 110, 119, 127, 135, 144) cm] bust circumference, and 19 ¾ (20 ¾, 21 ½, 22 ½, 23 ½, 24 ½, 25 ½, 26 ½)" [50 (53, 54.5, 57, 59.5, 62, 65, 67.5) cm] in length from back neck to hem
Sample shown is 33 ¼" [84.5 cm] with 3 ¼" [8.25 cm] positive ease

## Yarn
Sparrow by Quince & Co.
(100% organic linen; 168yd [155m]/50g)
• 5 (6, 7, 7, 8, 8, 9, 10) skeins in Birch 202
  Or 850 (925, 1025, 1125,1225, 1325, 1450, 1550) yds of fingering weight yarn

## Needles
• One 24" circular (circ) in size US 4 [3.5 mm]
• One 32" circ in size US 4 [3.5 mm] (optional)
## Or size to obtain gauge
## Notions
• Stitch markers (m)
• Stitch holders or waste yarn
• Tapestry needle
## Gauge
24 sts and 36 rows = 4" [10 cm] in stockinette stitch, after blocking.

## Tank
### Begin at the top
With shorter circ and using the long-tail cast on, CO 102 (104, 106, 108, 110, 112, 114, 116) sts, place marker (pm), CO 102 (104, 106, 108, 110, 112, 114, 116) sts. Place marker and join for working in the rnd, being careful not to twist sts—204 (208, 212, 216, 220, 224, 228, 232) sts.

Work in St st for 3 rnds.

**Next rnd** *dec row:* (K1, ssk, knit to 3 sts from m, k2tog, k1, sl m) two times (4 sts dec'd)—200 (204, 208, 212, 216, 220, 224, 228) sts.
Rep *dec row* every 4 rnds eight more times—168 (172, 176, 180, 184, 188, 192, 196) sts: 84 (86, 88, 90, 92, 94, 96, 98) front and back sts.

Work even for 3 rnds.

**Next rnd** *inc rnd:* K1, M1L, knit to last st before m, M1R, k1, sl m, knit to end (2 sts inc'd)—170 (174, 178, 182, 186, 190, 194, 198) sts.
Rep *inc rnd* every 4 rnds eight more times—186 (190, 194, 198, 202, 206, 210, 214) sts: 102 (104, 106, 108, 110, 112, 114, 116) front sts, 84 (86, 88, 90, 92, 94, 96, 98) back sts.

Knit 1 rnd.

## Front
**Next row:** Knit to m, turn. Place remaining sts on holder for back.
**Next row:** (WS) Purl.
**Next row** *inc row:* (RS) K1, M1L, knit to 1 st from end, M1R, k1 (2 sts inc'd)—104 (106, 108, 110, 112, 114, 116, 118).
Rep *inc row* every 4 rows 5 (5, 6, 6, 7, 7, 8, 8) more times—114 (116, 120, 122, 126, 128, 132, 134) sts.

**Set up row 1:** (RS) Knit to 12 (12, 13, 13, 14, 14, 15, 15) sts from end, pm, knit to end.
**Set up row 2:** (WS) Purl to 12 (12, 13, 13, 14, 14, 15, 15) sts from end, pm, purl to end.

**Next row** *dec row:* (RS) Knit to m, sl m, ssk, knit to 2 sts from m, k2tog, sl m, knit to end (2 sts dec'd)—112 (114, 118, 120, 124, 126, 130, 132) sts.
Rep *dec row* every RS row 14 (14, 15, 15, 16, 16, 17, 17) more times—84 (86, 88, 90, 92, 94, 96, 98) sts.

**At the same time,** when armhole measures 6 (6 ¼, 6 ½, 6 ¾, 7, 7 ¼, 7 ½, 7 ¾)" [15 (16, 16.5, 17, 18, 18.5, 19, 19.5) cm] begin armhole shaping:

**Next row** *inc row:* (RS) K1, M1L, work to 1 st from end, M1R, k1 (2 sts inc'd).
Rep *inc row* every RS row 2 (3, 4, 5, 6, 7, 8, 9) more times—90 (94, 98, 102, 106, 110, 114, 118) sts.
**Next row:** (WS) Purl.

Place sts on stitch holder or waste yarn.

## Back
Place 84 (86, 88, 90, 92, 94, 96, 98) back sts onto needle, ready to work a WS row.

Work in St st until armhole measures 6 (6 ¼, 6 ½, 6 ¾, 7, 7 ¼, 7 ½, 7 ¾)" [15 (16, 16.5, 17, 18, 18.5, 19, 19.5) cm].

**Next row** *inc row:* (RS) K1, M1L, work to 2 sts from end, M1R, k1(2 sts inc'd)—86 (88, 90, 92, 94, 96, 98, 100).
Rep *inc row* every RS row 2 (3, 4, 5, 6, 7, 8, 9) more times—90 (94, 98, 102, 106, 110, 114, 118) sts.
**Next row:** (WS) Purl.

## Join front and back
**Next rnd:** K90 (94, 98, 102, 106, 110, 114, 118) back sts, using the backward loop, CO 5 (8, 11, 14, 17, 20, 23, 26) sts, pm, CO 5 (8, 11, 14, 17, 20, 23, 26) sts, k90 (94, 98, 102, 106, 110, 114, 118) front sts, using the backward loop, CO 5 (8, 11, 14, 17, 20, 23, 26) sts, pm, CO 5 (8, 11, 14, 17, 20, 23, 26) sts—200 (220, 240, 260, 280, 300, 320, 340) sts.

Work in St st until body measures 3 (3, 3 ½, 3 ½, 4, 4, 4 ½, 4 ½)" [7.5 (7.5, 9, 9, 10, 10, 11.5, 11.5) cm] from underarm.

**Next rnd** *dec rnd:* (K1, ssk, knit to 3 sts from m, k2tog, k1, sl m) two times (4 sts dec'd)—196 (216, 236, 256, 276, 296, 316, 336) sts.
Work 3" [7.5 cm] even in St st, then rep *dec rnd* one more time—192 (212, 232, 252, 272, 292, 312, 332) sts.

Work in St st for 1" [2.5 cm].

**Next rnd** *inc rnd:* (K1, M1L, knit to 1 st from m, M1R, k1, sl m) two times (4 sts inc'd)— 196 (216, 236, 256, 276, 296, 316, 336) sts.

Work 3" [7.5 cm] even in St st, then rep *inc rnd* one more time—200 (220, 240, 260, 280, 300, 320, 340) sts.

Work even until body measures 13 (13 ½, 14, 14 ½, 15, 15 ½, 16, 16 ½)" [33 (34.5, 35.5, 37, 38, 39.5, 40.5, 42) cm] from underarm or desired length.

**Next rnd:** Bind off loosely.

## Finishing
Weave in all ends. Block to measurements.

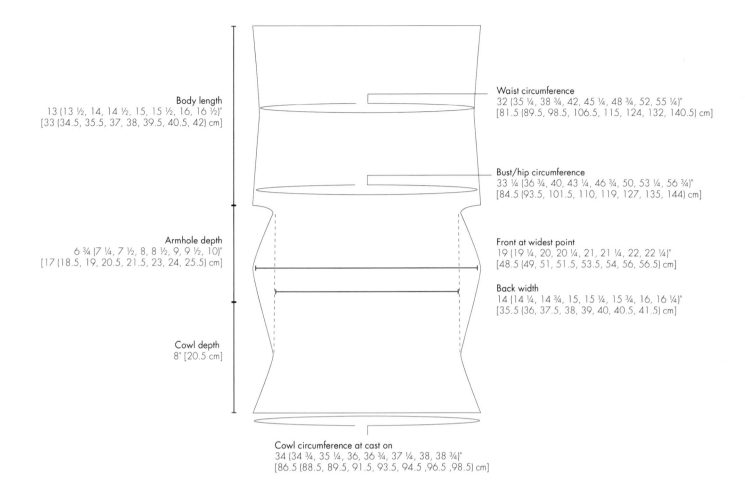

Body length
13 (13 ½, 14, 14 ½, 15, 15 ½, 16, 16 ½)"
[33 (34.5, 35.5, 37, 38, 39.5, 40.5, 42) cm]

Waist circumference
32 (35 ¼, 38 ¾, 42, 45 ¼, 48 ¾, 52, 55 ¼)"
[81.5 (89.5, 98.5, 106.5, 115, 124, 132, 140.5) cm]

Bust/hip circumference
33 ¼ (36 ¾, 40, 43 ¼, 46 ¾, 50, 53 ¼, 56 ¾)"
[84.5 (93.5, 101.5, 110, 119, 127, 135, 144) cm]

Armhole depth
6 ¾ (7 ¼, 7 ½, 8, 8 ½, 9, 9 ½, 10)"
[17 (18.5, 19, 20.5, 21.5, 23, 24, 25.5) cm]

Front at widest point
19 (19 ¼, 20, 20 ¼, 21, 21 ¼, 22, 22 ¼)"
[48.5 (49, 51, 51.5, 53.5, 54, 56, 56.5) cm]

Back width
14 (14 ¼, 14 ¾, 15, 15 ¼, 15 ¾, 16, 16 ¼)"
[35.5 (36, 37.5, 38, 39, 40, 40.5, 41.5) cm]

Cowl depth
8" [20.5 cm]

Cowl circumference at cast on
34 (34 ¾, 35 ¼, 36, 36 ¾, 37 ¼, 38, 38 ¾)"
[86.5 (88.5, 89.5, 91.5, 93.5, 94.5 ,96.5 ,98.5) cm]

# Put a Lid on It

This one-size-fits-all hat is designed to slouch at the top. Simple in stockinette stitch, a comfortable cap for transitional seasons and perhaps even summer itself.

### Finished measurements
22 ½" [57 cm] at brim and 10" [25.5 cm] from brim to crown
### Yarn
Sparrow by Quince & Co.
(100% organic linen; 168yd [155m]/50g)
- 2 skeins in Port 207
  Or 200 yds of fingering weight yarn
### Needles
- One 16" circular needle (circ) in size US 4 [3.5 mm]
- One set double-pointed needles (dpns) in size  US 4 [3.5 mm]
### Notions
- Stitch marker (m)
- Tapestry needle
### Gauge
24 sts and 36 rnds = 4" [10 cm] in stockinette stitch, after blocking.

## Hat
With circ and using the long-tail cast on, CO 135 sts. Join for working in the rnd, being careful not to twist sts. Place marker at beg of rnd.

Work in St st for 8 ½" [21.5 cm].

**Next rnd** *place markers*: *K9, pm; rep from * to last 9 sts, k9.
**Next rnd** *dec rnd*: *Knit to 2 sts before m, k2tog; rep from * to end (15 sts dec'd)—120 sts.
Rep *dec rnd* every other rnd 6 more times—30 sts rem.

Knit 1 rnd.

**Next rnd** *dec rnd*: *K2tog; rep from *—15 sts rem.

## Finishing
Cut yarn leaving a long tail. Thread tail onto tapestry needle, thread through remaining sts. Pull tight, weave end into WS of hat. Block to measurements.

# abbreviations

| | |
|---|---|
| beg | begin(ning); begin; begins |
| BO | bind off |
| CO | cast on |
| circ | circular needle |
| cm | centimeter(s) |
| cont | continue(s); continuing |
| dec('d) | decrease(d) |
| dpn(s) | double-pointed needle(s) |
| EOR | every other row/rnd |
| est | establish(ed) |
| g | gram(s) |
| inc('d) | increase(d) |
| k | knit |
| LH | left hand |
| mm | millimeter(s) |
| m(s) | marker(s) |
| p | purl |
| pm | place marker |
| rem | remain(ing) |
| rep | repeat; repeating |
| RH | right hand |
| rnd(s) | round(s) |
| RS | right side |
| sl m | slip marker |
| st(s) | stitch(es) |
| St st | stockinette stitch |
| WS | wrong side |
| yd(s) | yard(s) |

**M1R (make 1 right slanting):** Insert LH needle from back to front under horizontal strand between st just worked and next st, knit lifted strand through the front loop (1 st increased).

**M1L (make 1 left slanting):** Insert LH needle from front to back under horizontal strand between st just worked and next st, knit lifted strand through the back loop (1 st increased).

**ssk (slip, slip, knit):** Slip 2 sts one at a time knitwise to the RH needle; return sts to LH needle in turned position and knit them together through the back loops (1 st decreased, leans to the left).

**k2tog:** Knit 2 sts together (1 st decreased, leans to the right).

**ch (chain):** Wrap the yarn around the crochet hook (yarn over) and draw it through the loop on the hook to form the first chain. Rep this step as many times as instructed.

## Stockinette stitch (St st)
**Flat**
Knit on the RS and purl on the WS.
**In the round**
Knit every round.

## Techniques*
### Backward loop cast on
*Wrap yarn around left thumb from front to back and secure in palm with other fingers.w Insert needle upwards through strand on thumb. Slip loop from thumb onto RH needle, pulling yarn to tighten. Rep from * for desired number of sts.

## Long tail cast on
This cast on is so named for the long tail of yarn that is woven together with working yarn attached to the ball. Leaving a long tail, make a slip knot and place on right needle.
Note: it's better to overestimate how long the tail should be, depending on number of stitches to be cast on. With thumb and index finger of left hand, create a V by running working yarn over index finger and tail over thumb, palm facing upward. Bring needle up through loop created by thumb, catch the strand of the V running over index finger and go back down through loop created by thumb. Drop loop created by thumb, then using tail pull thumb back into V, tightening stitch created on needle.

*Video tutorials are available at knitbot.com

# bios

## Hannah Fettig
designs knitwear in Portland, Maine. She is the author of *Closely Knit*, *Knitbot Essentials*, and co-author of *Coastal Knits*, the smash self-published hit released in fall 2011. Her designs have also appeared in *Interweave Knits*, *Knitscene*, *Knitty*, and *Wool People*. You can view her full line of Knitbot patterns and obtain wholesale information at www.knitbot.com.

## Quince & Co
is the result of many "Wouldn't it be great if…" conversations among two knitwear designers and the owner of a spinning mill. We each confess to a strong bias toward natural fibers. In 2010, we combined efforts to create a line of thoughtfully conceived quality yarns spun from American wool or sourced from overseas suppliers who grow plants, raise animals, or manufacture a yarn in as earth- and labor-friendly a way as possible. Our linen yarn, Sparrow, is spun in Italy from fiber grown organically in Belgium, home of the finest linen fabrics in the world. www.quinceandco.com

# contributors

styling  Hannah Fettig

consultant  Pam Allen

shoot assistant  Jerusha Robinson

photographer & graphic designer  Carrie Bostick Hoge

location  Black Point Inn

model  Abigail Abraira-Burklin

book printing  Puritan Press

technical editors  Tana Pageler & Jerusha Robinson